Alligators

NATURE'S PREDATORS

Stuart A. Kallen and P. M. Boekhoff

KidHaven Press, an imprint of Gale Group, Inc.
P.O. Box 289009, San Diego, CA 92198-9009

Library of Congress Cataloging-in-Publication Data

Kallen, Stuart A., 1955–
    Alligators / by Stuart A. Kallen and Patti Marlene Boekhoff.
      p. cm. — (Nature's Predators)
    Includes bibliographical references (p.   )
    Summary: Discusses the evolutionary development of alligators, their physical structure, habitat, and mating and hunting habits. Also included is a discussion of the threat man poses to the species
    ISBN 0-7377-0642-2 (hardback : alk. paper)
    1. Alligators—Juvenile literature. [1. Alligators.]
    I. Boekhoff, P. M. (Patti Marlene), 1957– II. Title. III. Series.
    QL666.C925 K36 2002
    597.98'4—dc21

2001001439

Copyright 2002 by KidHaven Press, an imprint of Gale Group, Inc.
P. O. Box 289009, San Diego, CA 92198-9009

No part of this book may be reproduced or used in any other form or by any other means, electrical, mechanical, or otherwise, including, but not limited to, photocopying, recording, or any information storage and retrieval system, without prior written permission from the publisher.

Contents

Chapter 1: Armor-Plated Alligators 5

Chapter 2: Catching and Killing Prey 21

Chapter 3: Hunting the Hunters 32

Glossary 43

For Further Exploration 44

Index 46

Picture Credits 48

Chapter 1

Armor-Plated Alligators

Alligators are part of an ancient **species** that has roamed the earth nearly unchanged for more than 65 million years. They are living relatives of ancient reptiles such as dinosaurs and flying pterosaurs.

Today there are two species of alligator. *Alligator sinensis*, one of the most endangered reptiles in the world, lives in the marshes of the Yangtze River in China. Only about 150 of the animals are left in the wetlands near the heavily populated province of Anhui.

The American alligator, or *Alligator mississipiensis*, has a much broader range. It swims in waters from the southern tip of Florida up north to Virginia, west to Louisiana and the Rio Grande, and in the branches of the Mississippi River as far north as Oklahoma. When sixteenth-century Spanish explorers first came to the

This Chinese alligator is one of the most endangered reptiles in the world.

region, they called the animal a lizard—*el lagarto* in Spanish, or *alligator* in English.

While there are only several thousand alligators in most southeastern states, at least 1 million of the animals live in the wild in Florida, with the greatest concentration in Everglades National Park, where the alligator is known as the King of the Everglades.

Eating and Sleeping

Alligators can live on land but prefer water and may be found in marshes, swamps, ponds, drainage canals, and water-filled ditches. Alligators will eat anything that they can outswim, overpower, or ambush. And they will add to their diet with any dead animals they can find. An alligator's appetite can vary greatly. During times of low activity or cold weather, an alligator can eat less than five pounds of food per day—about the same amount as a large bird. An adult alligator can live up to a year with no food at all.

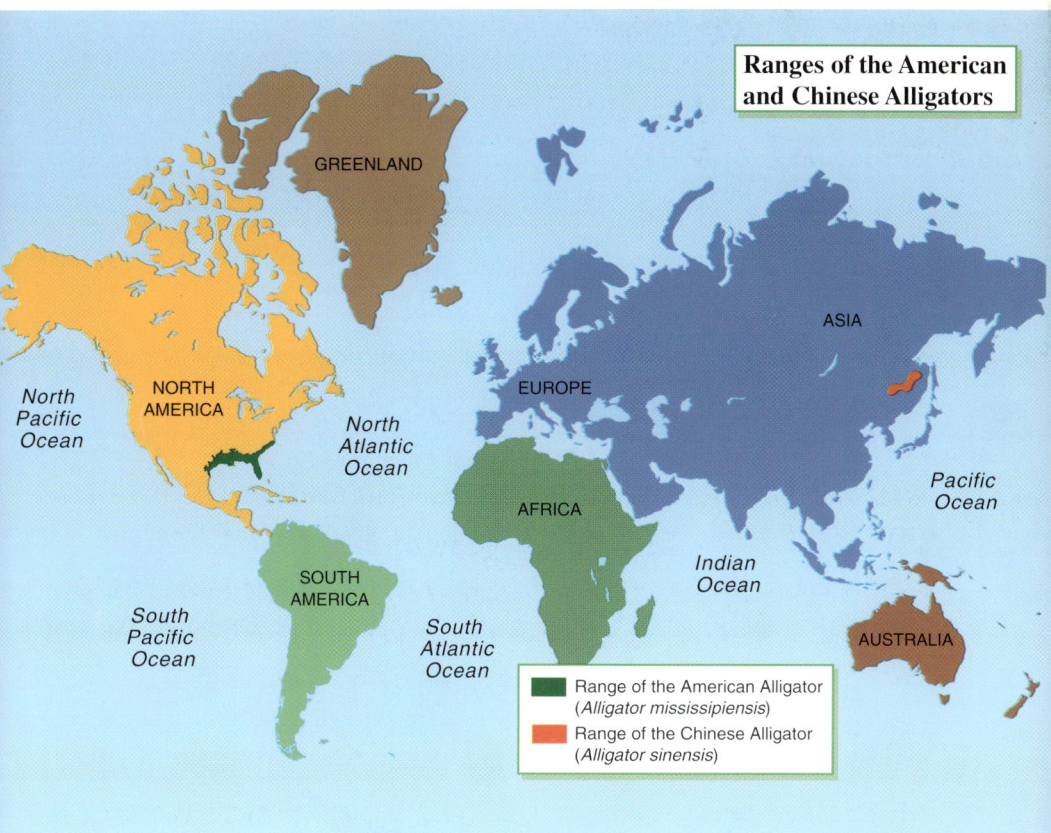

In spite of their big appetites, alligators do not need to eat during the winter, when they sleep for days at a time. Cool weather under seventy degrees slows their breathing and heartbeat. During this time the animals need little oxygen and may stay underwater for days. Alligators also stop eating during this period of semihibernation, waking only on warm days to hunt.

While American alligators live in tropical climates, their Chinese counterparts live in a cooler region on a latitude equal to the state of Maryland. These animals burrow into the ground and hibernate between October and April to escape winter temperatures.

Not a Crocodile

Although alligators are related to crocodiles, alligators look slightly different. Alligators are larger than crocodiles and have wide U-shaped noses. Crocodiles have pointy V-shaped snouts.

The animals also differ in the way their teeth come together. The upper jaw of the alligator is wider than the lower jaw, so the teeth of the animal's lower jaw are completely hidden when the mouth is closed. In crocodiles the lower and upper jaws are about the same size, and the teeth of both jaws fit together in an interlocking pattern.

Like the crocodile, the alligator's jaws have incredible crushing power, and the animals can

One of the differences between alligators (left) and crocodiles (right) is the shape of their snouts. Alligators' snouts are U-shaped and crocodiles' are V-shaped.

splinter cow bones and crush turtle shells. But this power only works when the alligator closes his jaws. The animal has much less power opening his mouth: An alligator's jaws can be easily held together by a person using both hands.

Designed to Kill

From the flashing white points of its eighty teeth to the very tip of its swishing green tail, the American alligator's body is designed to kill. Male alligators, called bulls, average twelve feet when fully grown, with their muscular tails accounting for half their body length. Weighing five hundred pounds, bull alligators are one of the world's largest reptiles and the biggest **predator** in the southern wetlands.

To reach such a size, alligators grow very rapidly and continue to grow throughout their lives. Although they are only about 7 inches long when they are born, baby alligators grow to 5 feet in length in the first six years of life. Females soon reach an average length of 8 feet. Old bulls may

Baby alligators are only about 7 inches long when they are born.

An alligator's back is covered with bony plates called scutes, made from the same material as human fingernails.

grow to 19 feet long and weigh 1,000 pounds during an average life span of thirty or more years.

The long, muscular alligator body is armor plated with thick scaly skin that no animal can penetrate with teeth or claws. The skin on the alligator's back is covered with bony plates called **scutes** that are made from the same hard material as human fingernails.

Unlike its big, ferocious American cousin, the Chinese alligator is a small and timid animal that weighs little more a hundred pounds. Although they look like American alligators, males rarely grow to more than six feet in length. This is only about half the size of American alligators.

11

This alligator is high walking, using its legs to travel while keeping its body off the ground.

All-Terrain Creatures

American alligators are large, but they move quickly through water, mud, or dirt. On land alligators have three separate methods of travel. In the belly crawl motion, the animal slithers across mud using its legs on the sides of its body rather than underneath. When the animal wants to chase down dinner, it can shift to the belly run motion and move across muddy terrain at about eight miles per hour—about as fast as a human can run.

If the alligator needs to travel over rough surfaces such as rocks and dry dirt, it can rise up and walk with its legs underneath its body. This action is known as a high walk and resembles the erect gait of a mammal. Alligators are the only reptiles that can travel in this manner.

To gain traction on any surface, alligators can dig into the ground with five sharp claws on their front feet and four long claws on their back feet. The three inner toes on the back feet have extra strong claws for pushing power. American alligators have webbing between their toes to help them walk through the mud without sinking.

Alligators use the claws on their feet to gain traction on any surface.

Chinese alligators, however, do not have this webbing between their toes.

Graceful Swimmers

While alligators can move fairly well on land, when they enter water, they become swift and graceful swimmers. The animals wriggle their powerful tails to move them forward while tucking their short front legs back into their bodies. The outstretched back legs and webbing between the toes act as rudders that stabilize the animal and allow it to steer. With this method, alligators can swim up to six miles per hour and remain underwater for fifteen minutes at a time.

To hide from **prey** while swimming, alligators swim slightly below the surface. And they can change colors to match the hue of the surrounding water. Those that live in clear streams and marshes turn bright green to blend in with the nearby trees, swamp grasses, and bushes. Alligators that reside in murky lowland streams called bayous take on a yellowish cast. Black alligators live in the Mississippi swamps, where the water is made dark by tupelo tree leaves, berries, and roots. Chinese alligators—known in China as *Tu Long*, or "muddy dragon"—are dark green to black and blend into the brackish waters of their swampy homes.

With their eyes, ears, and nostrils on top of the head, alligators can see, hear, and breathe while submerged.

Keen Senses

While its body blends into the scenery, the alligator's eyes, ears, and nostrils rise slightly above the water. Positioned on top of the head, these sense organs enable the animal to see, hear, and breathe when almost totally submerged.

Alligators have highly developed senses to give them a great advantage over most of their prey. They can detect the slightest motion with their big eyes and can see well in the dark.

Alligator eyes are highly reflective and glow in the night. The eyes of adult males glint red, while females' eyes glow greenish or bluish yellow. During the day the alligator's eyes contract into slit-like pupils, which shut out bright sunlight.

The alligator's sense of smell is so keen that it can pick up the smell of approaching prey long before the victims can see it. And alligators can hear animals drawing near from a great distance.

When alligators swim below the surface, their senses are somewhat dulled. To keep out water, valves close over their ears, nostrils, and windpipes. Special see-through lids close to protect their eyes while still allowing them to see, but their vision is blurred by the lid.

Three Thousand Teeth

Once an alligator sees a victim, it will lunge to capture its prey in a blur of white gnashing teeth. Alligators have thirty-eight to forty sharp teeth in the upper jaw, and the same number in the lower jaw. The front teeth are pointed for catching and holding prey. A large fourth tooth in the lower jaw acts as an extra hook for holding on to struggling prey.

Alligators' back teeth are rounded and used for crushing and dismembering prey that cannot be swallowed whole. Some back teeth in the lower jaw are slanted backward to help move larger

Alligators have seventy-six to eighty teeth that they use to catch and crush their prey.

prey into a position to be swallowed. When trying to eat big animals, the alligator may spin its body or violently shake its head to break off pieces small enough to swallow. If a chunk is still too large to get down the throat, the alligator will simply hold the food in its mouth until it decays to the point that it can be swallowed.

While catching and crushing prey, alligators constantly lose their teeth. These are quickly replaced, however, by replacement teeth, which

Alligators do not chew their food. Instead, they use their teeth to catch and tear their meals into pieces small enough to swallow.

sprout under the animal's gums. In this manner, an average alligator can go through two thousand to three thousand teeth in a lifetime.

Grinding Gizzards

Although they are very sharp, alligator teeth are made for grabbing and tearing, not for chewing. Instead, food is broken down in the alligator's stomach by very powerful digestive juices.

After being softened by the juices, the victim's body moves to the gizzard, a thick-walled muscular crushing chamber of the stomach that does the work of chewing the food. Alligators rely on hard pebbles such as quartz or granite to aid in this task. The stones are swallowed and line the animal's gizzard.

Catching and tearing apart prey is hard on an alligator's teeth. When a tooth is lost another one grows in.

If hard stones are not available, alligators will swallow bits of broken glass, tin cans, hard wood, shotgun shells, or even golf balls in order to make gizzard stones. These objects churn and grind against the swallowed prey, crushing it down to a pulp. This action allows alligators to completely digest the toughest parts of prey such as bones, hair, feathers, and scales.

With its tough stomach, keen senses, and armor-plated skin, the American alligator is an awesome predator whose entire body is finely tuned to hunt and eat. Sometimes called the last living dinosaurs, alligators are a reminder of the ferocious nature of life in prehistoric times.

Chapter 2

Catching and Killing Prey

Alligators are cunning hunters whose primary feeding time is at night. Full-grown American alligators eat a variety of animals such as large fish, waterbirds, turtles, snakes, small mammals such as deer, and even smaller alligators. The Chinese alligator also hunts mainly at night, feeding on snails and mussels as well as fish, frogs, and rats. Unlike American alligators, they rarely eat larger animals.

Feeding Their Babies

Baby American alligators eat crawfish, crabs, and reptiles such as frogs. Even when very small, they can leap out of the water to catch dragonflies and other insects.

Until they are about eighteen months old, the mother alligator offers them larger creatures,

This alligator has captured a duck. Alligators will eat a variety of animals.

capturing and crushing fish, turtles, and snakes. Once the prey is crushed, the mother holds it at the water's surface and allows her offspring to gather bits of flesh to eat. Like adults, baby alligators hold food in their small jaws and shake their heads to tear off little bits, raising their heads to gulp down the meat.

Catching Fish

American alligators have developed a wide variety of hunting methods to capture prey on land or in water. Since the animals are water-loving creatures and spend much of their time submerged, fish are the main source of alligator meals.

In places such as Florida's Everglades National Park, the alligator has quite a menu to choose from. There are over thirty species of fish that the animal can feed on, including mosquito fish, snapper, bluegill, and largemouth bass.

When fishing for a meal, the alligator uses several tricks to trap or stalk unsuspecting prey. The alligator's greatest weapon is its ability to lie very still for hours at a time, practically invisible to passing creatures. When a school of fish come within striking range, the alligator leaps out of the water and lands with a splash. As the surprised and confused fish scatter, the alligator shakes its head from side to side, snapping them up in a frenzy and swallowing them whole.

If an alligator finds a twenty-pound largemouth bass, it cannot swallow the fish in one gulp. Instead, the animal will take the bass onshore, swing it around, bash it on the ground until it is dead, then crush the fish up with its teeth. As the alligator throws its head up in the air, the pulverized bass slides down into its gizzard.

One of the alligator's favorite foods is the giant garfish, which grows up to five feet in length and can weigh more than thirty-five pounds. Like the

If an alligator catches a fish too big to swallow whole, it will bring the fish to shore to crush it into pieces small enough to swallow.

alligator, the gar is armor plated and a great predator, easily gobbling up many types of fish, including bass and bream. The alligator is the gar's only natural enemy. Without alligators keeping a check on their numbers, garfish would eat nearly every other fish in the Everglades.

Trapping Fish

While alligators sometimes battle thirty-pound garfish, they have also developed fishing methods where they herd small fish together with their tails. When an alligator wants to fish in this manner, it lays its head on a sandbar and curls its long tail into the current of a river. As the water pushes the prey into this trap, the alligator occasionally gives a sweeping swat with its tail and throws the fish up onto the riverbank, where they can be eaten later. The tail-in-the-river method works well when there are a limited number of fish and the alligator catches them alone.

In spring, when large schools of fish fill the wetlands, alligators catch fish together. Using a **technique** called cooperative feeding, the giant reptiles gather at a narrow part of a creek where it flows into a lake or pond. The alligators line up side by side in a row, facing the oncoming current and forming a living dam across the waterway. As the water flow carries the fish toward them, the alligators simply open their jaws, leaving no gaps in between for the fish to escape. If one alligator moves out of line, another one takes its place. After the biggest alligators have eaten their fill, the smaller animals are allowed to eat.

Alligators will normally fight over fish. During cooperative feeding, however, they feed so intensely that they seem to not notice anything else around them. By working cooperatively, the alligators can devour thousands of fish at a time. And they will return to their formation several times in one night if large schools of fish are nearby.

Attracting Prey to the Gator Hole

Cooperative feeding is used when there are large numbers of fish to be eaten. During the long, hot summers, however, extensive droughts dry up wetlands and sometimes kill up to 80 percent of the fish in places such as the Everglades. During these periods the alligator creates an oasis, called a gator hole, where fish can survive and provide food.

The alligator creates the gator hole by using its feet and snout to dig a deep pond from four to

An alligator creates a gator hole to attract other animals.

six feet deep and twelve feet across. These mini-swamps attract fish, turtles, snails, and other freshwater animals that move right in with alligators. While alligators feed on the prey concentrated in their gator holes, enough of the creatures survive to repopulate the region when the waters return to a wider area in autumn.

Snacking on Turtles and Snakes

Gator holes attract many species of turtles. The female red-bellied turtle sneaks into the gator hole and lays her eggs right in with the alligator eggs. Although the turtle is sometimes caught in the act, the shells of red-bellied turtles are so strong, they can withstand the bite of an angry alligator.

The shells of other turtles are not as strong, however. Slow-swimming Florida box turtles, peninsula cooters, and other turtles are easy game for the alligator. People who live near the Everglades can sometimes hear the loud cracking sound of alligators shattering turtle shells late at night.

Gator holes also attract many types of snakes from the two-foot-long brown water snake to the indigo snake, which can grow to eight feet in length. Alligators will eat any snake swimming or slithering by and instinctively know which ones are poisonous. Harmless snakes such as the brown water snake are simply swallowed whole headfirst.

Poisonous snakes such as the six-foot-long diamondback rattler can engage an alligator in a

The red-bellied turtle is one of the many animals attracted to gator holes.

dramatic battle. While the snake strikes the alligator again and again, the rattler's poisonous fangs are no match for the alligator's scaly armor. The alligator simply grabs the snake in its powerful jaws and crunches it down the entire length of its body. Finally, throwing the dead animal up in the air and catching it, the alligator swallows the snake whole. Although the alligator may have taken several poisonous bites to the tongue, the giant predator is not harmed by snake venom.

Snakes, fish, and baby turtles also provide food for wading birds, such as the ibis, heron, stork, snowy egret, and spoonbill. These birds sometimes fall prey to lunging alligators that float like logs in the gator hole.

Killing Deer

While the water in the gator hole provides a **habitat** for snakes and turtles, it also attracts larger animals that come to quench their thirst. Mammals such as marsh rabbits, foxes, raccoons, opossums, and white-tail deer are often seen around the gator hole.

When a deer bends down to sip water out of a hole, the alligator may surprise it with an explosive attack. Jumping more than five feet straight up out of the water, the alligator snaps its powerful jaws around the nose of the frightened deer. Trapped on the steep, slippery mud, the deer cannot run away.

In the grip of the alligator's sharp teeth, the deer is pulled, shaken, and jerked into the water. The pain in the sensitive nerves of the deer's nostrils and lips is so great that the animal will often surrender and walk into the water. The alligator then flips the unfortunate animal over and holds it underwater until it drowns.

If the animal struggles, the alligator will use its strong tail to spin in the water, rolling and twisting its body with great power. The alligator holds the prey in its jaws and thrashes it violently until it is dead. If the victim is too large to be swallowed whole, the alligator tears it apart. It can crush the leg bones of the deer with one quick snap of its giant jaws. Holding the animal in its long rows of pointed teeth, the alligator can rip the legs loose from the body by twisting, shaking, and rolling.

Kingdom of the Alligator

The gator hole has allowed alligators to become successful predators because of their ability to

An alligator will tear large prey into pieces by twisting, shaking, rolling, and spinning in the water.

control the environment in which they live. By providing a home for itself, the alligator also gives hundreds of animals a place to find food and water. Without gator holes, the survival of some of these animals, such as wading birds and turtles, would be threatened.

Alligators may be fierce predators that mercilessly kill whatever they can catch, but these massive reptiles and their gator holes also play an important part in preserving the environment. Without the King of the Everglades, thousands of animals would perish and the wild kingdom of the alligator could not exist.

Chapter 3

Hunting the Hunters

Adult American alligators are the top predators in their environment and have few natural enemies. Alligator eggs and baby alligators, however, are eaten by many creatures. As a result, female alligators fiercely protect their young for at least two years after they are born.

To insure the survival of her eggs, a female alligator constructs a mounded nest from wetland vegetation. She lays from thirty-five to eighty eggs in the heat of the summer, between late June and early July. For the next sixty-five days, until the eggs are hatched, the female stays nearby. Using her keen senses, she guards against raccoons, bears, and other predators that may try to steal her eggs.

Protecting Hatchlings

When the baby alligators are ready to hatch, they make high-pitched grunting sounds. This warns the mother to remove the nesting material that covers the eggs.

When the seven-inch-long hatchlings break out of their eggs, they are fully formed but helpless. The mother remains nearby ready to fight off predators, such as wading birds, bobcats,

Female alligators will lay between thirty-five and eighty eggs during the summer.

Baby alligators make grunting noises as they hatch, letting the mother alligator know it is time to uncover the eggs.

otters, snakes, large bass, and even other alligators.

To warn away intruders, the female can inflate her body to appear larger than it really is. When predators approach, she will hiss, roar, and lunge forward while whacking her tail hard on the ground.

If the predator is another alligator, a brutal battle of gnashing jaws may result. The animals will use their tails as levers to get their jaws into position to bite. Once a female has the leg or tail of an enemy caught in her deadly jaws, she will try to twist it off by quickly rolling over and over. If the two opponents lock their jaws together, each will try to twist the other's head off. In such a case, a female will fight to the death to protect her young.

Despite her protective instincts, however, the female cannot possibly guard the dozens of hatchlings that are born at one time. During the first two years of life, eight out of ten baby alligators will fall victim to predators.

Growing Human Threat

Once alligators grow to four feet in length, they are safe from every predator except human beings. People have been hunting alligators for their meat and skins for centuries.

While most of the alligator's skin is tough and scaly, the soft, white underbelly of the animal is ideal for making shoes, purses, coats, and other items. As early as 1800, alligator skins were sold in Miami for $7 each. This was a large sum at the time, and it attracted hundreds of alligator hunters to Florida.

By the end of the nineteenth century, the population of Florida was growing at a rapid pace. Those who did not hunt alligators considered them a deadly nuisance. In the 1890s, the state of Florida ordered the widespread slaughter of alligators

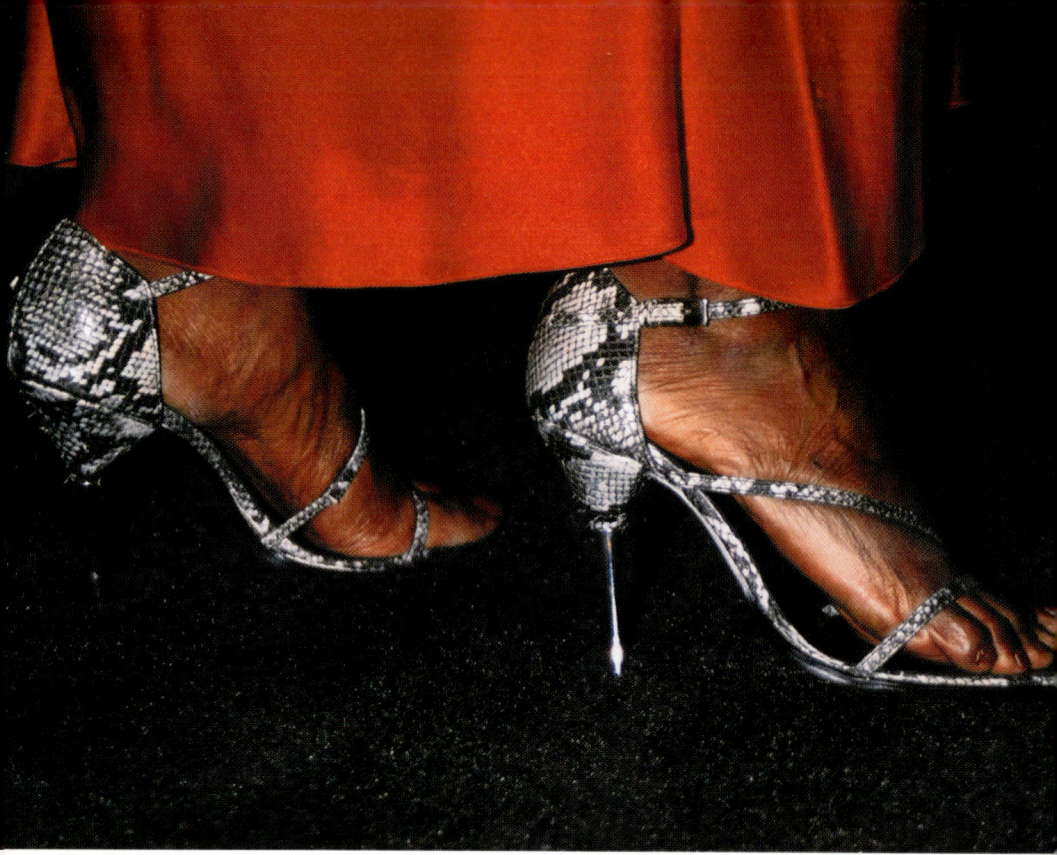

Humans have hunted alligators for centuries and used their skins to make items such as the shoes pictured here.

because they were seen as a threat to fishermen, ranchers, and other settlers. In 1891 alone more than 2.5 million alligators were killed in Florida. Throughout the twentieth century, at least 150,000 alligator hides were taken every year.

Hunting Alligators

Although they were widely killed, alligators are clever creatures that are not easily trapped. People have developed many tricks over the years, however, to catch them. For instance, alligators are easiest to catch at night when they are out hunting. Their bright eyes glowing above the water make them easy targets for hunters, who blind them with spotlights and shoot them.

Other hunters use the gator call, in which they imitate the cry of a wounded or frightened

Alligators are easily caught at night, when they can be blinded by bright lights.

alligator. This sound is made by grunting "umph, umph, umph" in a high key with the lips closed. Alligators who hear this will come to help or to see what the danger is. When an alligator draws near, it can be easily killed.

Hunters also capture alligators with baited hooks. The hook is baited with a cow heart or an entire dead chicken and dangled on a rope about a foot above the water. When the alligator leaps up to take the bait, it becomes ensnared on the hook, thrashing helplessly out of the water. At this time it can be shot by a hunter, who hides in nearby bushes.

Alligators can also be hunted while they hide in their gator holes. Fearless hunters have been known to reach into gator holes, grab an animal's snout, and pull it out by its nose. Other hunters use a long pole twelve to eighteen feet long, with a large, sharp iron hook on the end. This pole is poked into gator holes until the enraged creature bites the hook. Once its sharp teeth are clamped around the pole, the hunter can pull the alligator out of its lair.

To avoid hunters while hiding in gator holes, alligators dig tunnels six feet below the surface with multiple exits. When humans are nearby, alligators can disappear into a maze of tunnels and caves that stretch up to sixty feet away from the hole.

Alligators also have long memories and are hard to fool twice. If an animal escapes a blinding spotlight, it will disappear underwater the next time one approaches. If it should struggle free from a baited hook, it will try to avoid such a trap in the future.

Protecting Alligators

Although alligators have developed several survival strategies, they could not outsmart their

Many laws are now in place to protect alligators and help the species survive.

39

human enemies in the long run. By the middle of the twentieth century, American alligators were nearly wiped out in many parts of the Southeast. In the 1940s restrictions were placed on hunting the animals, but poachers continued to kill alligators illegally. In 1973 alligators were declared an endangered species and given greater protection under federal law.

Once they received protection, alligator populations began to rebound rapidly. By the 1980s there were so many alligators that they became a nuisance to citizens in Florida. Alligators began crawling into people's backyards and hiding under their cars. To quell the exploding population, alligators were taken off the endangered species list in 1983.

In 1984 several states began to allow hunting of alligators. The hunts, however, were strictly limited, with only 2,500 to 3,000 of the animals allowed to be killed in the wild every year. With this small number of animals taken, the alligator population grew to more than 1.5 million animals in Florida and Louisiana.

Today almost all alligators used for meat and leather are raised on special farms. In 2000 Louisiana had the most alligator farms, with 122 licensed facilities. Florida had 42 alligator farms; Texas, 40; Georgia, 7; Mississippi, 5; and Alabama, only 2. In that year alone, the alligator farms produced more than 35,000 feet of skins and 406,000 pounds of meat at a value of nearly $6 million.

Threats Remain

While the alligator population grows, human threats to the animal remain. In 2000 the state of Florida had a population of 12.5 million people that was increasing by 900 a day. As a result, alligators continue to lose habitat to homes, businesses, and shopping centers.

In addition, the natural flow of water in the Everglades has been radically changed by dams

Alligator farms, such as this one in Florida, help balance the survival of the animal with the commercial needs for its skin and meat.

and irrigation projects. During times of drought, the water is diverted to the human population and gator holes disappear. Alligators survive by crowding together in the few remaining holes. Without fish, snakes, turtles, and deer, the alligators are forced to eat each other. The disappearance of gator holes has also affected another of the alligator's favorite foods, wading birds, whose populations have been reduced by 90 percent from historic levels.

Water diverted for human use is also polluted by toxic chemicals from factories, farms, power plants, and incinerators. Pollution from sewage runoff, herbicides, and pesticides is now among the greatest threats to alligators.

Alligators' Ancient Home

Alligators have thrived in wild wetlands for millions of years—long before human beings walked the earth. As relatives to ancient dinosaurs, the animals have one foot in the prehistoric past and one foot in the modern age. While humans remain the biggest threat to alligators today, they are also among their strongest supporters. With careful **conservation** of their ancient watery homes, alligators will remain the top predators in the southern swamps for a long time to come.

Glossary

conserve: To keep from being lost, damaged, or wasted.

habitat: The place where a plant or animal naturally grows and lives.

predator: A creature that lives by killing and eating other creatures.

prey: An animal hunted or caught for food.

quarry: An animal that is being hunted.

scutes: Bony plates on the alligator's back made from the same hard material as human fingernails.

species: A category or group of related plants or animals.

technique: A method of carrying out a plan.

For Further Exploration

Books

Jim Arnosky, *All About Alligators*. New York: Scholastic, 1994.
> A colorful book that describes the physical characteristics and behavior of various members of the crocodilian family.

Sabrina Crewe, *The Alligator*. Austin, TX: Raintree Steck-Vaughn, 1998.
> A simple introduction to the life cycle, physical characteristics, behavior, and habitat of the American alligator.

Allan Fowler, *Gator or Croc?* Danbury, CT: Children's Press, 1996.
> A simple book that shows the differences between alligators and crocodiles.

Louise Martin, *Alligators*. Vero Beach, FL: Rourke Enterprises, 1989.
> A book that describes the physical characteristics of alligators, and how they find food, mate, and raise their young.

John Woodward, *Crocodiles & Alligators*. New York: Benchmark Books, 1999.
> From the Endangered! series, this book examines the physical characteristics, behavior, and life cycle of crocodiles and alligators, and discusses their endangered status.

Websites

Crocodilians Natural History & Conservation. www.flmnh.ufl.edu/natsci/herpetology/brittoncrocs/cnhc.html.
> An alligator and crocodile site that provides in-depth information about different species, biology, and even their captive care.

Natural Wildlife Federation, Ranger Rick's Homepage. www.nwf.org/rrick/.
> A fun website that provides articles about the problems alligators are facing due to destruction of their habitats. Alligator articles may be found by going to the search page and typing in "alligators."

The University of Florida Institute of Food and Agricultural Sciences AgriGator. www.ifas.ufl.edu/AgriGator/gators/.
> An informative website that provides information about alligator populations, habitats in Florida, reproduction, feeding habits, value of meat and hides, alligators and humans, and living with alligators, along with photos and other information.

Index

Alligator mississipiensis, 5
Alligator sinensis, 5
alligators
  American
    babies, 10, 21–22
    habitat of, 5
    mothers, 32–35
    number of, 6
    prey of, 23–24
    semihibernation of, 8
    size of, 9–11
    toes of, 13–14
  Chinese
    habitat of, 5
    hibernation of, 8
    size of, 11
    toes of, 14
appetite, 7–8
armor plate, 11

babies
  enemies of, 32, 33–34, 35
  feeding of, 21–22
  size of, 10
bass, 23
bears, 32

belly running, 12
birds, 18–19, 42
body
  armor plate, 11
  claws, 13
  jaws, 8–9, 29–30
  noses, 8
  skin, 35
  stomachs, 18–20
  tails, 29
  teeth, 9, 16–18, 29
  toes, 13–14
bulls, 9–11

camouflage, 14
claws, 13
crocodiles, 8–9

deer, 29–30
digestion, 18–20
dinosaurs, 5, 42
drought, 26, 42

enemies
  animals, 32, 33–34, 35
  humans, 35–38, 40
Everglades National Park, 6, 23

farms, 40
feeding, 25–26
fish, 23–24
Florida
  hunting alligators in, 35–36, 40
  loss of habitat in, 41–42

garfish, 23–24
gator calls, 37–38
gator holes
  alligators hunted in, 38
  described, 26–27, 38
  disappearance of, 42
  importance of, 30–31
  prey and, 27–30
gizzards, 19–20

habitat, 5, 6–7, 41–42
hatchlings, 33–34
hearing, 16
hunting methods
  belly running, 12
  gator holes, 27–31
  herding, 25
  killing of prey, 17, 23
  stalking, 23
  swimming, 14, 16
  teeth and, 16–18

jaws, 8–9, 29–30

King of the Everglades, 6

mothers
  feed babies, 21–22

protect babies, 32–35

noses, 8

poachers, 40
prey, 21
  dead animals, 7
  deer, 29–30
  fish, 23–24
  snakes, 28
  turtles, 27–28
  wading birds, 29, 42
protection, 39–40

raccoons, 32

scutes, 11
sight, 15–16
skin, 35
sleep, 8
slithering, 12
smell, 16
snakes, 28
species, 5
speed, 12, 14
stomachs, 18–20
swimming, 14, 16

tails, 29
teeth, 9, 16–18, 29
toes, 13–14
travel 12–14
turtles, 27–28

walking, 13
weather, 8, 26, 42

47

Picture Credits

Cover Photo: © Art Wolfe/Photo Researchers Inc.
Animals Animals © Joe McDonald, 22
Animals Animals © S. Osolinski, 19
Animals Animals © Lynn M. Stone, 18
© Kevin Fleming/Corbis, 37
© F. Gohier, 1982/Photo Researchers Inc., 26
© Philip Gould/Corbis, 33
© David Hosking/Photo Researchers Inc., 24, 39
© George Kleiman/Photo Researchers Inc., 30
© Danny Lehman/Corbis, 9
© S. R. Maglione, 1996/Photo Researchers Inc., 41
© John-Marshall Mantel/Corbis, 36
© W. M. Munoz, 1993/Photo Researchers Inc., 13
© National Zoological Park, Tom McHugh, 1972/Photo Researchers Inc., 6
© Stan Osolinski, 1992/FPG International, 15
© Stan Osolinski, 1997/FPG International, 17
© Robt. H. Potts Jr./Photo Researchers Inc., 34
Martha E. Schierholz, 7
© M. H. Sharp, 1992/Photo Researchers Inc., 12
© Kennan Ward/Corbis, 10
© Jeanne White/Photo Researchers Inc., 12
© Jim Zipp, 1999/Photo Researchers Inc., 28